Bible Promises
for
Peace on
Earth

Bible Promises
for
Peace on Earth

*Hundreds of Encouraging Scriptures
Arranged by Topic*

BARBOUR
PUBLISHING

© 2013 by Barbour Publishing, Inc.

Compiled by Russell A. Wight

Print ISBN 978-1-62416-189-6

All scripture quotations are taken from the King James Version of the Bible.

Cover image © Sandralise/veer.com

Published by Barbour Publishing, Inc., P.O. Box 719, Uhrichsville, Ohio 44683, www.barbourbooks.com

Our mission is to publish and distribute inspirational products offering exceptional value and biblical encouragement to the masses.

 Member of the
Evangelical Christian
Publishers Association

Printed in the United States of America.

Contents

Introduction

To everything there is a season,
and a time to every purpose under the heaven:
A time to be born, and a time to die;
a time to plant, and a time to pluck up
that which is planted;
a time to kill, and a time to heal;
a time to break down, and a time to build up;
a time to weep, and a time to laugh;
a time to mourn, and a time to dance;
a time to cast away stones,
and a time to gather stones together;
a time to embrace, and a time
to refrain from embracing;
a time to get, and a time to lose;
a time to keep, and a time to cast away;
a time to rend, and a time to sew;
a time to keep silence, and a time to speak;
a time to love, and a time to hate;
a time of war, and a time of peace.

ECCLESIASTES 3:1–8

How we long to live in a time of peace and a time of love. But, too often, it seems our world is only consumed with hate and war. Where can we seek peace in these troubled times?

The answer is, of course, with the God of heaven—

the God who has revealed Himself through His Son Jesus Christ (the living Word) and the Holy Bible (the written Word). Through the scriptures, we learn that God the Father has sent His Holy Spirit to live within those who believe in Jesus, so that they may all experience peace while living in a world at war.

May the portions of the Word of God found on the following pages be a blessing to you as you seek peace through our Lord Jesus Christ.

The
Biblical
Promise
of
Peace

How beautiful upon the mountains are the feet of
him that bringeth good tidings, that publisheth peace;
that bringeth good tidings of good, that publisheth
salvation; that saith unto Zion, Thy God reigneth!
ISAIAH 52:7

Adam and Eve were placed into a world at peace—
but that peace was destroyed by a serpent and by
sin. God promised the fallen couple a descendent
who would bring the defeat of the serpent and the
forgiveness of sin, thus restoring peace.

This promised descendent would eventually
come to earth as a baby—born in humble surround-
ings in Bethlehem, announced to a collection of
shepherds by a multitude of the heavenly host.

Glory to God in the Highest, and on earth peace,
good will toward men.

11

The Christmas Story

And it came to pass in those days, that there went out a decree from Caesar Augustus that all the world should be taxed. (And this taxing was first made when Cyrenius was governor of Syria.) And all went to be taxed, every one into his own city. And Joseph also went up from Galilee, out of the city of Nazareth, into Judaea, unto the city of David, which is called Bethlehem; (because he was of the house and lineage of David:) To be taxed with Mary his espoused wife, being great with child. And so it was, that, while they were there, the days were accomplished that she should be delivered. And she brought forth her firstborn son, and wrapped him in swaddling clothes, and laid him in a manger; because there was no room for them in the inn. And there were in the same country shepherds abiding in the field, keeping watch over their flock by night. And, lo, the angel of the Lord came upon them, and the glory of the Lord shone round about them: and they were sore afraid. And the angel said unto them, Fear not: for, behold, I bring you good tidings of great joy, which shall be to all people. For unto you is born this day in the city of David a Saviour, which is Christ the Lord. And this shall be a sign unto you; Ye shall find the babe wrapped in swaddling clothes, lying in a manger. And suddenly there was with the angel a multitude of the heavenly host praising God, and saying, Glory to God in the highest, and on earth peace, good will toward men. And it came to pass, as the angels were gone away from them into heaven, the shepherds said one to another, Let us now go even unto Bethlehem, and see this thing which is come to pass, which the Lord hath made known unto us. And they came with haste, and found Mary, and Joseph, and the babe lying in a manger. And when they had seen it, they made known abroad the saying which was told them concerning this child.

LUKE 2:1–17

This baby did not enjoy peace in His time on earth. He was despised and rejected, and eventually was crucified on a cross on a hill called Calvary. The Christmas story turned into the Easter story, with the God-Man rising from the dead to conquer death and sin.

The Easter Story

Who hath believed our report? and to whom is the arm of the Lord revealed? For he shall grow up before him as a tender plant, and as a root out of a dry ground: he hath no form nor comeliness; and when we shall see him, there is no beauty that we should desire him. He is despised and rejected of men; a man of sorrows, and acquainted with grief: and we hid as it were our faces from him; he was despised, and we esteemed him not. Surely he hath borne our griefs, and carried our sorrows: yet we did esteem him stricken, smitten of God, and afflicted. But he was wounded for our transgressions, he was bruised for our iniquities: the chastisement of our peace was upon him; and with his stripes we are healed. All we like sheep have gone astray; we have turned every one to his own way; and the Lord hath laid on him the iniquity of us all. He was oppressed, and he was afflicted, yet he opened not his mouth: he is brought as a lamb to the slaughter, and as a sheep before her shearers is dumb, so he openeth not his mouth. He was taken from prison and from judgment: and who shall declare his generation? for he was cut off out of the land of the living: for the transgression of my people was he stricken. And he made his grave with the wicked, and with the rich in his death; because he had done no violence, neither was any deceit in his mouth. Yet it pleased the Lord to bruise him; he hath put him to grief: when thou shalt make his soul an offering for sin, he shall see his seed, he shall prolong his days, and the pleasure of the Lord shall prosper in his hand. He shall see of the travail of his soul, and shall be satisfied: by his knowledge shall my righteous servant justify many; for he shall bear their iniquities. Therefore will I divide him a portion with the great, and he shall divide the spoil with the strong; because he hath poured out his soul unto death: and he was numbered with the transgressors; and he bare the sin of many, and made intercession for the transgressors.

ISAIAH 53:1–12

This risen man now sits at the right hand of God and will one day return to this world to establish an everlasting kingdom of peace.

The Kingdom Story

For the kingdom of God is not meat and drink; but righteousness, and peace, and joy in the Holy Ghost. For he that in these things serveth Christ is acceptable to God, and approved of men. Let us therefore follow after the things which make for peace, and things wherewith one may edify another.

ROMANS 14:17–19

And the God of peace shall bruise Satan under your feet shortly.

ROMANS 16:20

And I saw a new heaven and a new earth: for the first heaven and the first earth were passed away; and there was no more sea. And I John saw the holy city, new Jerusalem, coming down from God out of heaven, prepared as a bride adorned for her husband. And I heard a great voice out of heaven saying, Behold, the tabernacle of God is with men, and he will dwell with them, and they shall be his people, and God himself shall be with them, and be their God. And God shall wipe away all tears from their eyes; and there shall be no more death, neither sorrow, nor crying, neither shall there be any more pain: for the former things are passed away.

REVELATION 21:1–4

O Jesus, my Savior,
All glory to Thee;
Sweet peace in believing
Thou givest to me.

Refrain
Peace, peace to my soul
Flows like a beautiful river;
Peace, hallowed and pure,
Constant abiding forever.

FANNY CROSBY

At
Peace
with
God

*Elect according to the foreknowledge of God
the Father, through sanctification of the Spirit,
unto obedience and sprinkling of the blood of Jesus
Christ: Grace unto you, and peace, be multiplied.*
1 PETER 1:2

There is no greater goal in life for the mortal man to
be at peace with God. The Bible presents the Father,
the Son, and the Holy Spirit as the givers of peace.

The Father

The LORD will give strength unto his people; the LORD will bless his people with peace.

PSALM 29:11

As for me, I will call upon God; and the LORD shall save me. Evening, and morning, and at noon, will I pray, and cry aloud: and he shall hear my voice. He hath delivered my soul in peace from the battle that was against me: for there were many with me. God shall hear, and afflict them, even he that abideth of old. Selah. Because they have no changes, therefore they fear not God. He hath put forth his hands against such as be at peace with him: he hath broken his covenant. The words of his mouth were smoother than butter, but war was in his heart: his words were softer than oil, yet were they drawn swords. Cast thy burden upon the LORD, and he shall sustain thee: he shall never suffer the righteous to be moved.

PSALM 55:16–22

I will hear what God the LORD will speak: for he will speak peace unto his people, and to his saints: but let them not turn again to folly.

PSALM 85:8

For the mountains shall depart, and the hills be removed; but my kindness shall not depart from thee, neither shall the covenant of my peace be removed, saith the LORD that hath mercy on thee.

ISAIAH 54:10

And the peace of God, which passeth all understanding, shall keep your hearts and minds through Christ Jesus.

PHILIPPIANS 4:7

Those things, which ye have both learned, and received, and heard, and seen in me, do: and the God of peace shall be with you.

Philippians 4:9

Rest in the Lord, and wait patiently for him: fret not thyself because of him who prospereth in his way, because of the man who bringeth wicked devices to pass.

Psalm 37:7

Now the God of peace, that brought again from the dead our Lord Jesus, that great shepherd of the sheep, through the blood of the everlasting covenant, Make you perfect in every good work to do his will, working in you that which is wellpleasing in his sight, through Jesus Christ; to whom be glory for ever and ever. Amen.

Hebrews 13:20–21

LORD, thou wilt ordain peace for us: for thou also hast wrought all our works in us.

ISAIAH 26:12

I am the LORD, and there is none else, there is no God beside me: I girded thee, though thou hast not known me: That they may know from the rising of the sun, and from the west, that there is none beside me. I am the LORD, and there is none else. I form the light, and create darkness: I make peace, and create evil: I the LORD do all these things.

ISAIAH 45:5–7

My soul, wait thou only upon God; for my expectation is from him. He only is my rock and my salvation: he is my defence; I shall not be moved.

PSALM 62:5–6

He maketh peace in thy borders, and filleth thee with the finest of the wheat.

PSALM 147:14

And of whom hast thou been afraid or feared, that thou hast lied, and hast not remembered me, nor laid it to thy heart? have not I held my peace even of old, and thou fearest me not?

ISAIAH 57:11

I create the fruit of the lips; Peace, peace to him that is far off, and to him that is near, saith the LORD; and I will heal him.

ISAIAH 57:19

The glory of this latter house shall be greater than of the former, saith the LORD of hosts: and in this place will I give peace, saith the LORD of hosts.

HAGGAI 2:9

. . .but glory, honour, and peace, to every man that worketh good, to the Jew first, and also to the Gentile: For there is no respect of persons with God.

ROMANS 2:10–11

For God is not the author of confusion, but of peace, as in all churches of the saints.

1 CORINTHIANS 14:33

Peace, troubled soul, thou need'st not fear;
Thy great Provider still is near;
Who fed thee last, will feed thee still:
Be calm, and sink into His will.

The Lord, who built the earth and sky,
In mercy stoops to hear thy cry;
His promise all may freely claim;
Ask and receive in Jesus' Name.

SAMUEL ECKING

The Son

For unto us a child is born, unto us a son is given: and the government shall be upon his shoulder: and his name shall be called Wonderful, Counsellor, The mighty God, The everlasting Father, The Prince of Peace. Of the increase of his government and peace there shall be no end, upon the throne of David, and upon his kingdom, to order it, and to establish it with judgment and with justice from henceforth even for ever. The zeal of the LORD OF HOSTS WILL PERFORM THIS.

ISAIAH 9:6–7

Give the king thy judgments, O God, and thy righteousness unto the king's son. He shall judge thy people with righteousness, and thy poor with judgment. The mountains shall bring peace to the people, and the little hills, by righteousness. He shall judge the poor of the people, he shall save the children of the needy, and shall break in pieces the oppressor. They shall fear thee as long as the sun and moon endure, throughout all generations. He shall come down like rain upon the mown grass: as showers that water the earth. In his days shall the righteous flourish; and abundance of peace so long as the moon endureth.

PSALM 72:1–7

But he was wounded for our transgressions, he was bruised for our iniquities: the chastisement of our peace was upon him; and with his stripes we are healed.

ISAIAH 53:5

But thou, Bethlehem Ephratah, though thou be little among the thousands of Judah, yet out of thee shall he come forth unto me that is to be ruler in Israel; whose goings forth have been from of old, from everlasting. Therefore will he give them up, until the time that she which travaileth hath brought forth: then the remnant of his brethren shall return unto the children of Israel. And he shall stand and feed in the strength of the LORD, in the majesty of the name of the LORD his God; and they shall abide: for now shall he be great unto the ends of the earth. And this man shall be the peace.

MICAH 5:2–5

And the word of the LORD came unto me, saying, Take of them of the captivity, even of Heldai, of Tobijah, and of Jedaiah, which are come from Babylon, and come thou the same day, and go into the house of Josiah the son of Zephaniah; Then take silver and gold, and make crowns, and set them upon the head of Joshua the son of Josedech, the high priest; And speak unto him, saying, Thus speaketh the LORD of hosts, saying, Behold the man whose name is The BRANCH; and he shall grow up out of his place, and he shall build the temple of the LORD: Even he shall build the temple of the LORD; and he shall bear the glory, and shall sit and rule upon his throne; and he shall be a priest upon his throne: and the counsel of peace shall be between them both.

ZECHARIAH 6:9–13

Whosoever therefore shall confess me before men, him will I confess also before my Father which is in heaven. But whosoever shall deny me before men, him will I also deny before my Father which is in heaven. Think not that I am come to send peace on earth: I came not to send peace, but a sword.

MATTHEW 10:32–34

Suppose ye that I am come to give peace on earth? I tell you, Nay; but rather division: For from henceforth there shall be five in one house divided, three against two, and two against three. The father shall be divided against the son, and the son against the father; the mother against the daughter, and the daughter against the mother; the mother in law against her daughter in law, and the daughter in law against her mother in law.

LUKE 12:51–53

Now the chief priests, and elders, and all the council, sought false witness against Jesus, to put him to death; But found none: yea, though many false witnesses came, yet found they none. At the last came two false witnesses, And said, This fellow said, I am able to destroy the temple of God, and to build it in three days. And the high priest arose, and said unto him, Answerest thou nothing? what is it which these witness against thee? But Jesus held his peace, And the high priest answered and said unto him, I adjure thee by the living God, that thou tell us whether thou be the Christ, the Son of God. Jesus saith unto him, Thou hast said: nevertheless I say unto you, Hereafter shall ye see the Son of man sitting on the right hand of power, and coming in the clouds of heaven.

MATTHEW 26:59–64

Therefore being justified by faith, we have peace with God through our Lord Jesus Christ:

ROMANS 5:1

But now in Christ Jesus ye who sometimes were far off are made nigh by the blood of Christ. For he is our peace, who hath made both one, and hath broken down the middle wall of partition between us; Having abolished in his flesh the enmity, even the law of commandments contained in ordinances; for to make in himself of twain one new man, so making peace; And that he might reconcile both unto God in one body by the cross, having slain the enmity thereby: And came and preached peace to you which were afar off, and to them that were nigh. For through him we both have access by one Spirit unto the Father.

EPHESIANS 2:13–18

And, having made peace through the blood of his cross, by him to reconcile all things unto himself; by him, I say, whether they be things in earth, or things in heaven.

COLOSSIANS 1:20

Now the Lord of peace himself give you peace always by all means. The Lord be with you all.

2 THESSALONIANS 3:16

I saw the cross of Jesus,
    when burdened with my sin;
I sought the cross of Jesus,
    to give me peace within;
I brought my soul to Jesus,
    He cleansed it in His blood;
And in the cross of Jesus I found
    my peace with God.

Safe in the cross of Jesus!
    There let my weary heart
Still rest in peace unshaken,
    till with Him, ne'er to part;
And then in strains of glory I'll
    sing His wondrous power,
Where sin can never enter,
    and death is known no more.

FREDERICK WHITFIELD

The Holy Spirit

These things have I spoken unto you, being yet present with you. But the Comforter, which is the Holy Ghost, whom the Father will send in my name, he shall teach you all things, and bring all things to your remembrance, whatsoever I have said unto you. Peace I leave with you, my peace I give unto you: not as the world giveth, give I unto you. Let not your heart be troubled, neither let it be afraid. Ye have heard how I said unto you, I go away, and come again unto you. If ye loved me, ye would rejoice, because I said, I go unto the Father: for my Father is greater than I.

JOHN 14:25–28

For they that are after the flesh do mind the things of the flesh; but they that are after the Spirit the things of the Spirit. For to be carnally minded is death; but to be spiritually minded is life and peace.

ROMANS 8:5–6

For the kingdom of God is not meat and drink; but righteousness, and peace, and joy in the Holy Ghost. For he that in these things serveth Christ is acceptable to God, and approved of men. Let us therefore follow after the things which make for peace, and things wherewith one may edify another.

ROMANS 14:17–19

But the fruit of the Spirit is love, joy, peace, longsuffering, gentleness, goodness, faith, Meekness, temperance: against such there is no law.

GALATIANS 5:22–23

I therefore, the prisoner of the Lord, beseech you that ye walk worthy of the vocation wherewith ye are called, With all lowliness and meekness, with longsuffering, forbearing one another in love; endeavouring to keep the unity of the Spirit in the bond of peace. There is one body, and one Spirit, even as ye are called in one hope of your calling; One Lord, one faith, one baptism, One God and Father of all, who is above all, and through all, and in you all.

EPHESIANS 4:1–6

Holy Spirit, Peace divine,
Still this restless heart of mine;
Speak to calm this tossing sea,
Stayed in Thy tranquility.

Now incline me to repent,
Let me now my sins lament,
Now my foul revolt deplore,
Weep, believe, and sin no more.

SAMUEL LONGFELLOW

At
Peace
with
Myself

For to be carnally minded is death;
but to be spiritually minded
is life and peace.
ROMANS 8:6

The individual at peace with God must then exercise the spiritual disciplines to move to a place of peace within. Once that individual has assurance of salvation, the process of sanctification—spiritual growth—may fully take hold. Through the study of the Word of God, the confession of sin, and regular prayer, the Christian can experience peace in his or her heart.

Salvation

Mark the perfect man, and behold the upright: for the end of that man is peace.

PSALM 37:37

Thou wilt keep him in perfect peace, whose mind is stayed on thee: because he trusteth in thee.

ISAIAH 26:3

Therefore being justified by faith, we have peace with God through our Lord Jesus Christ.

ROMANS 5:1

For whosoever shall call upon the name of the Lord shall be saved. How then shall they call on him in whom they have not believed? and how shall they believe in him of whom they have not heard? and how shall they hear without a preacher? And how shall they preach, except they be sent? as it is written, How beautiful are the feet of them that preach the gospel of peace, and bring glad tidings of good things!

ROMANS 10:13–15

But now in Christ Jesus ye who sometimes were far off are made nigh by the blood of Christ. For he is our peace, who hath made both one, and hath broken down the middle wall of partition between us; Having abolished in his flesh the enmity, even the law of commandments contained in ordinances; for to make in himself of twain one new man, so making peace; And that he might reconcile both unto God in one body by the cross, having slain the enmity thereby: And came and preached peace to you which were afar off, and to them that were nigh. For through him we both have access by one Spirit unto the Father.

EPHESIANS 2:13–18

All glory be to Thee, Most High,
To Thee all adoration;
In grace and truth Thou drawest nigh
To offer us salvation;
Thou showest Thy good will to men,
And peace shall reign on earth again;
We praise Thy Name forever.

UNKNOWN

But of him are ye in Christ Jesus, who of God is made unto us wisdom, and righteousness, and sanctification, and redemption: That, according as it is written, He that glorieth, let him glory in the Lord.

1 CORINTHIANS 1:30–31

Sanctification

The steps of a good man are ordered by the Lord: and he delighteth in his way. Though he fall, he shall not be utterly cast down: for the Lord upholdeth him with his hand.

Psalm 37:23–24

My son, forget not my law; but let thine heart keep my commandments: For length of days, and long life, and peace, shall they add to thee.

Proverbs 3:1–2

But God forbid that I should glory, save in the cross of our Lord Jesus Christ, by whom the world is crucified unto me, and I unto the world. For in Christ Jesus neither circumcision availeth any thing, nor uncircumcision, but a new creature. And as many as walk according to this rule, peace be on them, and mercy, and upon the Israel of God.

Galatians 6:14–16

Finally, my brethren, be strong in the Lord, and in the power of his might. Put on the whole armour of God, that ye may be able to stand against the wiles of the devil. For we wrestle not against flesh and blood, but against principalities, against powers, against the rulers of the darkness of this world, against spiritual wickedness in high places. Wherefore take unto you the whole armour of God, that ye may be able to withstand in the evil day, and having done all, to stand. Stand therefore, having your loins girt about with truth, and having on the breastplate of righteousness; And your feet shod with the preparation of the gospel of peace; Above all, taking the shield of faith, wherewith ye shall be able to quench all the fiery darts of the wicked. And take the helmet of salvation, and the sword of the Spirit, which is the word of God: Praying always with all prayer and supplication in the Spirit, and watching thereunto with all perseverance and supplication for all saints.

EPHESIANS 6:10–18

Now no chastening for the present seemeth to be joyous, but grievous: nevertheless afterward it yieldeth the peaceable fruit of righteousness unto them which are exercised thereby.

HEBREWS 12:11

෨෫ඁ

And the fruit of righteousness is sown in peace of them that make peace.

JAMES 3:18

෨෫ඁ

Wherefore, beloved, seeing that ye look for such things, be diligent that ye may be found of him in peace, without spot, and blameless.

2 PETER 3:14

But of him are ye in Christ Jesus, who of God is made unto us wisdom, and righteousness, and sanctification, and redemption: That, according as it is written, He that glorieth, let him glory in the Lord.

1 CORINTHIANS 1:30–31

What a fellowship, what a joy divine,
Leaning on the everlasting arms;
What a blessedness, what a peace is mine,
Leaning on the everlasting arms.

Refrain
Leaning, leaning, safe and secure from
   all alarms;
Leaning, leaning, leaning on the
   everlasting arms.

ELISHA HOFFMAN

Contentment

Rest in the LORD, and wait patiently for him: fret not thyself because of him who prospereth in his way, because of the man who bringeth wicked devices to pass.

PSALM 37:7

But godliness with contentment is great gain. For we brought nothing into this world, and it is certain we can carry nothing out. And having food and raiment let us be therewith content.

1 TIMOTHY 6:6–8

Not that I speak in respect of want: for I have learned, in whatsoever state I am, therewith to be content.

PHILIPPIANS 4:11

Let your conversation be without covetousness; and be content with such things as ye have: for he hath said, I will never leave thee, nor forsake thee.

HEBREWS 13:5

Sweet the moments, rich in blessing,
Which before the cross we spend,
Life and health and peace possessing
From the sinner's dying Friend.

Here I stay, forever viewing
Mercy streaming in His blood;
Precious drops, my soul bedewing,
Plead and claim my peace with God.

Oh, that, near the cross abiding,
We may to the Savior cleave,
Naught with Him our hearts dividing,
All for Him content to leave!

JAMES ALLEN AND WALTER SHIRLEY

Prayer

Hear the voice of my supplications, when I cry unto thee, when I lift up my hands toward thy holy oracle. Draw me not away with the wicked, and with the workers of iniquity, which speak peace to their neighbours, but mischief is in their hearts. Give them according to their deeds, and according to the wickedness of their endeavours: give them after the work of their hands; render to them their desert. Because they regard not the works of the LORD, nor the operation of his hands, he shall destroy them, and not build them up. Blessed be the LORD, because he hath heard the voice of my supplications.

PSALM 28:2–6

Pray for the peace of Jerusalem: they shall prosper that love thee.

PSALM 122:6

And the very God of peace sanctify you wholly; and I pray God your whole spirit and soul and body be preserved blameless unto the coming of our Lord Jesus Christ.

1 THESSALONIANS 5:23

Deeper, deeper in the faith of Jesus,
Holy faith and true;
In His pow'r and soul exulting wisdom
Let me peace pursue.

Refrain
O deeper yet, I pray,
And higher every day,
And wiser, blessèd Lord,
In Thy precious, holy Word.

CHARLES P. JONES

Confession

O LORD my God, in thee do I put my trust: save me from all them that persecute me, and deliver me: Lest he tear my soul like a lion, rending it in pieces, while there is none to deliver. O Lord my God, If I have done this; if there be iniquity in my hands; If I have rewarded evil unto him that was at peace with me; (yea, I have delivered him that without cause is mine enemy:) Let the enemy persecute my soul, and take it; yea, let him tread down my life upon the earth, and lay mine honour in the dust. Selah.

PSALM 7:1–5

Great peace have they which love thy law: and nothing shall offend them.

PSALM 119:165

Behold, for peace I had great bitterness: but thou hast in love to my soul delivered it from the pit of corruption: for thou hast cast all my sins behind thy back.

ISAIAH 38:17

Jesus only can impart
Balm to heal the smitten heart;
Peace that flows from sin forgiven,
Joy that lifts the soul to Heaven.

Chief of sinners though I be,
Christ is all in all to me;
All my wants to Him are known,
All my sorrows are His own;

WILLIAM McCOMB

At
Peace
with
Others

Depart from evil, and do good;
seek peace, and pursue it.
PSALM 34:14

Blessed are the peacemakers:
for they shall be called the children of God.
MATTHEW 5:9

For Christians, there is no greater display of our peace with God than to live at peace in this world.

Every Christian has family and friends in this world with whom they live peacefully. And there is a greater community, as well, where the Christian interacts with neighbors and with government. But

Christians also find themselves confronted with enemies: enemies of God, who are also enemies of us as individual believers.

Whoever we have to deal with, the Bible gives clear direction for how to live in peace while we move through this temporary, fast-moving life.

At Home

I will both lay me down in peace, and sleep: for thou, Lord, only makest me dwell in safety.

PSALM 4:8

And all thy children shall be taught of the Lord; and great shall be the peace of thy children.

ISAIAH 54:13

For the unbelieving husband is sanctified by the wife, and the unbelieving wife is sanctified by the husband: else were your children unclean; but now are they holy. But if the unbelieving depart, let him depart. A brother or a sister is not under bondage in such cases: but God hath called us to peace. For what knowest thou, O wife, whether thou shalt save thy husband? or how knowest thou, O man, whether thou shalt save thy wife?

1 CORINTHIANS 7:14–16

Flee also youthful lusts: but follow righteousness, faith, charity, peace, with them that call on the Lord out of a pure heart.

2 TIMOTHY 2:22

What doth it profit, my brethren, though a man say he hath faith, and have not works? can faith save him? If a brother or sister be naked, and destitute of daily food, And one of you say unto them, Depart in peace, be ye warmed and filled; notwithstanding ye give them not those things which are needful to the body; what doth it profit? Even so faith, if it hath not works, is dead, being alone.

JAMES 2:14–17

Happy the home when God is there,
And love fills every breast;
When one their wish, and one their prayer,
And one their heav'nly rest.

Lord, let us in our homes agree
This blessed peace to gain;
Unite our hearts in love to Thee,
And love to all will reign.

HENRY WARE, JR.

At Work

Servants, be obedient to them that are your masters according to the flesh, with fear and trembling, in singleness of your heart, as unto Christ; Not with eyeservice, as menpleasers; but as the servants of Christ, doing the will of God from the heart; with good will doing service, as to the Lord, and not to men: Knowing that whatsoever good thing any man doeth, the same shall he receive of the Lord, whether he be bond or free. And, ye masters, do the same things unto them, forbearing threatening: knowing that your Master also is in heaven; neither is there respect of persons with him.

EPHESIANS 6:5–9

Servants, obey in all things your masters according to the flesh; not with eyeservice, as menpleasers; but in singleness of heart, fearing God:

COLOSSIANS 3:22

Servants, be subject to your masters with all fear; not only to the good and gentle, but also to the froward. For this is thankworthy, if a man for conscience toward God endure grief, suffering wrongfully.

1 PETER 2:18–19

Let as many servants as are under the yoke count their own masters worthy of all honour, that the name of God and his doctrine be not blasphemed.

1 TIMOTHY 6:1

Hark, the voice of Jesus calling,
"Who will go and work today?
Fields are ripe and harvests waiting,
Who will bear the sheaves away?"
Long and loud the Master calls us,
Rich reward He offers free;
Who will answer, gladly saying,
"Here am I, send me, send me"?

If you cannot be the watchman,
Standing high on Zion's wall,
Pointing out the path to heaven,
Offering life and peace to all,
With your prayers and with your
bounties
You can do what heaven demands;
You can be like faithful Aaron,
Holding up the prophet's hands.

DANIEL MARCH

At Church

But as God hath distributed to every man, as the Lord hath called every one, so let him walk. And so ordain I in all churches.

1 Corinthians 7:17

Obey them that have the rule over you, and submit yourselves: for they watch for your souls, as they that must give account, that they may do it with joy, and not with grief: for that is unprofitable for you.

Hebrews 13:17

Salt is good: but if the salt have lost his saltness, wherewith will ye season it? Have salt in yourselves, and have peace one with another.

Mark 9:50

For God is not the author of confusion, but of peace, as in all churches of the saints.

1 CORINTHIANS 14:33

Finally, brethren, farewell. Be perfect, be of good comfort, be of one mind, live in peace; and the God of love and peace shall be with you.

2 CORINTHIANS 13:11

I therefore, the prisoner of the Lord, beseech you that ye walk worthy of the vocation wherewith ye are called, with all lowliness and meekness, with long-suffering, forbearing one another in love; endeavouring to keep the unity of the Spirit in the bond of peace. There is one body, and one Spirit, even as ye are called in one hope of your calling; One Lord, one faith, one baptism, One God and Father of all, who is above all, and through all, and in you all.

EPHESIANS 4:1–6

And let the peace of God rule in your hearts, to the which also ye are called in one body; and be ye thankful.

COLOSSIANS 3:15

But of the times and the seasons, brethren, ye have no need that I write unto you. For yourselves know perfectly that the day of the Lord so cometh as a thief in the night. For when they shall say, Peace and safety; then sudden destruction cometh upon them, as travail upon a woman with child; and they shall not escape.

1 THESSALONIANS 5:1–3

And we beseech you, brethren, to know them which labour among you, and are over you in the Lord, and admonish you; and to esteem them very highly in love for their work's sake. And be at peace among yourselves.

1 THESSALONIANS 5:12–13

79

Finally, be ye all of one mind, having compassion one of another, love as brethren, be pitiful, be courteous: Not rendering evil for evil, or railing for railing: but contrariwise blessing; knowing that ye are thereunto called, that ye should inherit a blessing. For he that will love life, and see good days, let him refrain his tongue from evil, and his lips that they speak no guile: Let him eschew evil, and do good; let him seek peace, and ensue it. For the eyes of the Lord are over the righteous, and his ears are open unto their prayers: but the face of the Lord is against them that do evil.

1 Peter 3:8–12

O Church of God, arise!
The grand old choral strain
Of peace on earth, good will to man,
That rang on Judah's plain,
O'er all the world shall ring,
And echo far and wide,
And then the King, thy Lord, shall come,
And claim His faithful bride.

FANNY CROSBY

In Society

For my brethren and companions' sakes, I will now say, Peace be within thee.

PSALM 122:8

He that is void of wisdom despiseth his neighbour: but a man of understanding holdeth his peace.

PROVERBS 11:12

Deceit is in the heart of them that imagine evil: but to the counsellors of peace is joy.

PROVERBS 12:20

Their tongue is as an arrow shot out; it speaketh deceit: one speaketh peaceably to his neighbour with his mouth, but in heart he layeth his wait. Shall I not visit them for these things? saith the LORD: shall not my soul be avenged on such a nation as this?

JEREMIAH 9:8–9

And when ye come into an house, salute it. And if the house be worthy, let your peace come upon it: but if it be not worthy, let your peace return to you. And whosoever shall not receive you, nor hear your words, when ye depart out of that house or city, shake off the dust of your feet.

MATTHEW 10:12–14

After these things the LORD appointed other seventy also, and sent them two and two before his face into every city and place, whither he himself would come. Therefore said he unto them, The harvest truly is great, but the labourers are few: pray ye therefore the Lord of the harvest, that he would send forth labourers into his harvest. Go your ways: behold, I send you forth as lambs among wolves. Carry neither purse, nor scrip, nor shoes: and salute no man by the way. And into whatsoever house ye enter, first say, Peace be to this house. And if the son of peace be there, your peace shall rest upon it: if not, it shall turn to you again. And in the same house remain, eating and drinking such things as they give: for the labourer is worthy of his hire. Go not from house to house.

LUKE 10:1–7

Follow peace with all men, and holiness, without which no man shall see the Lord.

HEBREWS 12:14

The goodly land I see,
    with peace and plenty bless'd;
A land of sacred liberty,
    and endless rest.
There milk and honey flow,
    and oil and wine abound,
And trees of life forever grow
    with mercy crowned.

There dwells the Lord our King,
    the Lord our righteousness,
Triumphant o'er the world and sin,
    the Prince of peace;
On Sion's sacred height His kingdom
    still maintains,
And glorious with His saints
    in light forever reigns.

THOMAS OLIVERS

With Enemies

When a man's ways please the LORD, he maketh even his enemies to be at peace with him.

PROVERBS 16:7

I will give thee thanks in the great congregation: I will praise thee among much people. Let not them that are mine enemies wrongfully rejoice over me: neither let them wink with the eye that hate me without a cause. For they speak not peace: but they devise deceitful matters against them that are quiet in the land.

PSALM 35:18–20

If thou see the ass of him that hateth thee lying under his burden, and wouldest forbear to help him, thou shalt surely help with him.

EXODUS 23:5

In my distress I cried unto the LORD, and he heard me. Deliver my soul, O LORD, from lying lips, and from a deceitful tongue. What shall be given unto thee? or what shall be done unto thee, thou false tongue? Sharp arrows of the mighty, with coals of juniper. Woe is me, that I sojourn in Mesech, that I dwell in the tents of Kedar! My soul hath long dwelt with him that hateth peace. I am for peace: but when I speak, they are for war.

PSALM 120:1–7

If thine enemy be hungry, give him bread to eat; and if he be thirsty, give him water to drink.

PROVERBS 25:21

All glory to God in the sky,
And peace upon earth be restored!
O Jesus, exalted on high,
Appear our omnipotent Lord.

O wouldst Thou again be made known,
Again in Thy Spirit descend,
And set up in each of Thine own
A kingdom that never shall end!

Thou only art able to bless,
And make the glad nations obey,
And bid the dire enmity cease,
And bow the whole world to Thy sway.

CHARLES WESLEY

The
World
at
Peace

Seek the peace of the city
whither I have caused you
to be carried away captives,
and pray unto the Lord for it:
for in the peace thereof
shall ye have peace.
JEREMIAH 29:7

We do not need to list the places in our world where war and conflict are found. This problem will not be solved until Jesus Christ has returned to earth and reigns from an earthly throne.

Still, the Bible speaks to us about peace from the perspective of Israel and Jerusalem. It also uses the ancient kingdom of Babylon to instruct us regarding the various world governments that would follow.

Israel

And Moses said unto the people, Fear ye not, stand still, and see the salvation of the Lord, which he will shew to you to day: for the Egyptians whom ye have seen to day, ye shall see them again no more for ever. The Lord shall fight for you, and ye shall hold your peace.

EXODUS 14:13–14

So the Philistines were subdued, and they came no more into the coast of Israel: and the hand of the Lord was against the Philistines all the days of Samuel. And the cities which the Philistines had taken from Israel were restored to Israel, from Ekron even unto Gath; and the coasts thereof did Israel deliver out of the hands of the Philistines. And there was peace between Israel and the Amorites. And Samuel judged Israel all the days of his life.

1 SAMUEL 7:13–15

As for such as turn aside unto their crooked ways, the Lord shall lead them forth with the workers of iniquity: but peace shall be upon Israel.

PSALM 125:5

Blessed is every one that feareth the LORD; that walketh in his ways. For thou shalt eat the labour of thine hands: happy shalt thou be, and it shall be well with thee. Thy wife shall be as a fruitful vine by the sides of thine house: thy children like olive plants round about thy table. Behold, that thus shall the man be blessed that feareth the LORD. The LORD shall bless thee out of Zion: and thou shalt see the good of Jerusalem all the days of thy life. Yea, thou shalt see thy children's children, and peace upon Israel.

PSALM 128:1–6

For unto us a child is born, unto us a son is given: and the government shall be upon his shoulder: and his name shall be called Wonderful, Counsellor, The mighty God, The everlasting Father, The Prince of Peace. Of the increase of his government and peace there shall be no end, upon the throne of David, and upon his kingdom, to order it, and to establish it with judgment and with justice from henceforth even for ever. The zeal of the LORD of hosts will perform this.

ISAIAH 9:6–7

In that day the LORD with his sore and great and strong sword shall punish leviathan the piercing serpent, even leviathan that crooked serpent; and he shall slay the dragon that is in the sea. In that day sing ye unto her, A vineyard of red wine. I the Lord do keep it; I will water it every moment: lest any hurt it, I will keep it night and day. Fury is not in me: who would set the briers and thorns against me in battle? I would go through them, I would burn them together. Or let him take hold of my strength, that he may make peace with me; and he shall make peace with me. He shall cause them that come of Jacob to take root: Israel shall blossom and bud, and fill the face of the world with fruit.

ISAIAH 27:1–6

But Israel shall be saved in the LORD with an everlasting salvation: ye shall not be ashamed nor confounded world without end.

ISAIAH 45:17

Behold, I will bring it health and cure, and I will cure them, and will reveal unto them the abundance of peace and truth. And I will cause the captivity of Judah and the captivity of Israel to return, and will build them, as at the first.

JEREMIAH 33:6–7

Moreover I will make a covenant of peace with them; it shall be an everlasting covenant with them: and I will place them, and multiply them, and will set my sanctuary in the midst of them for evermore. My tabernacle also shall be with them: yea, I will be their God, and they shall be my people. And the heathen shall know that I the LORD do sanctify Israel, when my sanctuary shall be in the midst of them for evermore.

EZEKIEL 37:26–28

The word which God sent unto the children of Israel, preaching peace by Jesus Christ: (he is Lord of all:) That word, I say, ye know, which was published throughout all Judaea, and began from Galilee, after the baptism which John preached; How God anointed Jesus of Nazareth with the Holy Ghost and with power: who went about doing good, and healing all that were oppressed of the devil; for God was with him. And we are witnesses of all things which he did both in the land of the Jews, and in Jerusalem; whom they slew and hanged on a tree: Him God raised up the third day, and shewed him openly; Not to all the people, but unto witnesses chosen before God, even to us, who did eat and drink with him after he rose from the dead.

ACTS 10:36–41

Happy the man whose hopes rely
On Israel's God: He made the sky,
And earth, and seas, with all their train:
His truth for ever stands secure;
He saves th'oppressed, He feeds the poor,
And none shall find His promise vain.

The Lord has eyes to give the blind;
The Lord supports the sinking mind;
He sends the labr'ing conscience peace;
He helps the stranger in distress,
The widow, and the fatherless,
And grants the pris'ner sweet release.

ISAAC WATTS

Jerusalem

Pray for the peace of Jerusalem: they shall prosper that love thee.

PSALM 122:6

For Zion's sake will I not hold my peace, and for Jerusalem's sake I will not rest, until the righteousness thereof go forth as brightness, and the salvation thereof as a lamp that burneth. And the Gentiles shall see thy righteousness, and all kings thy glory: and thou shalt be called by a new name, which the mouth of the LORD shall name. Thou shalt also be a crown of glory in the hand of the Lord, and a royal diadem in the hand of thy God. Thou shalt no more be termed Forsaken; neither shall thy land any more be termed Desolate: but thou shalt be called Hephzibah, and thy land Beulah: for the Lord delighteth in thee, and thy land shall be married. For as a young man marrieth a virgin, so shall thy sons marry thee: and as the bridegroom rejoiceth over the bride, so shall thy God rejoice over thee. I have set watchmen upon thy walls, O Jerusalem, which shall never hold their peace day nor night: ye that make mention of the Lord, keep not silence, And give him no rest, till he establish, and till he make Jerusalem a praise in the earth.

ISAIAH 62:1–7

Hear the word of the LORD, ye that tremble at his word; Your brethren that hated you, that cast you out for my name's sake, said, Let the LORD be glorified: but he shall appear to your joy, and they shall be ashamed. A voice of noise from the city, a voice from the temple, a voice of the LORD that rendereth recompence to his enemies. Before she travailed, she brought forth; before her pain came, she was delivered of a man child. Who hath heard such a thing? who hath seen such things? Shall the earth be made to bring forth in one day? or shall a nation be born at once? for as soon as Zion travailed, she brought forth her children. Shall I bring to the birth, and not cause to bring forth? saith the LORD: shall I cause to bring forth, and shut the womb? saith thy God. Rejoice ye with Jerusalem, and be glad with her, all ye that love her: rejoice for joy with her, all ye that mourn for her: That ye may suck, and be satisfied with the breasts of her consolations; that ye may milk out, and be delighted with the abundance of her glory. For thus saith the LORD, Behold, I will extend peace to her like a river, and the glory of the Gentiles like a flowing stream: then shall ye suck, ye shall be borne upon her sides, and be dandled upon her knees.

ISAIAH 66:5–12

These are the things that ye shall do; speak ye every man the truth to his neighbour; execute the judgment of truth and peace in your gates: And let none of you imagine evil in your hearts against his neighbour; and love no false oath: for all these are things that I hate, saith the LORD. And the word of the LORD of hosts came unto me, saying, Thus saith the LORD of hosts; The fast of the fourth month, and the fast of the fifth, and the fast of the seventh, and the fast of the tenth, shall be to the house of Judah joy and gladness, and cheerful feasts; therefore love the truth and peace.

ZECHARIAH 8:16–19

And when he was come nigh, even now at the descent of the mount of Olives, the whole multitude of the disciples began to rejoice and praise God with a loud voice for all the mighty works that they had seen; Saying, Blessed be the King that cometh in the name of the Lord: peace in heaven, and glory in the highest. And some of the Pharisees from among the multitude said unto him, Master, rebuke thy disciples. And he answered and said unto them, I tell you that, if these should hold their peace, the stones would immediately cry out. And when he was come near, he beheld the city, and wept over it, Saying, If thou hadst known, even thou, at least in this thy day, the things which belong unto thy peace! but now they are hid from thine eyes.

LUKE 19:37–42

Lord, in this Thy mercy's day,
Ere for us it pass away,
On our knees we fall and pray.

By Thy tears of bitter woe,
For Jerusalem below,
Let us not Thy peace forego.

ISAAC WILLIAMS

Babylon

Thus saith the LORD, thy Redeemer, the Holy One of Israel; I am the LORD thy God which teacheth thee to profit, which leadeth thee by the way that thou shouldest go. O that thou hadst hearkened to my commandments! then had thy peace been as a river, and thy righteousness as the waves of the sea: Thy seed also had been as the sand, and the offspring of thy bowels like the gravel thereof; his name should not have been cut off nor destroyed from before me. Go ye forth of Babylon, flee ye from the Chaldeans, with a voice of singing declare ye, tell this, utter it even to the end of the earth; say ye, The LORD hath redeemed his servant Jacob. And they thirsted not when he led them through the deserts: he caused the waters to flow out of the rock for them: he clave the rock also, and the waters gushed out. There is no peace, saith the LORD, unto the wicked.

ISAIAH 48:17–22

Thus saith the LORD of hosts, the God of Israel, unto all that are carried away captives, whom I have caused to be carried away from Jerusalem unto Babylon; Build ye houses, and dwell in them; and plant gardens, and eat the fruit of them; Take ye wives, and beget sons and daughters; and take wives for your sons, and give your daughters to husbands, that they may bear sons and daughters; that ye may be increased there, and not diminished. And seek the peace of the city whither I have caused you to be carried away captives, and pray unto the LORD for it: for in the peace thereof shall ye have peace.

JEREMIAH 29:4–7

Oh, how beautiful their feet
    upon the mountains,
The tidings of peace who bring,
    who bring,
To the nations of the earth
    who sit in darkness,
And tell them of Zion's King:

Let the distant isles be glad,
Let them hail the Savior's birth,
And the news of pardon free,
Till the knowledge of the truth
Shall extend to all the earth,
As the waters o'er the sea.

FANNY CROSBY

Other
Aspects
of
Peace

Grace, mercy, and peace,
from God our Father
and Jesus Christ our Lord.
1 TIMOTHY 1:2

In many reference books, peace is a topic that stands on its own. Often in the Bible, the word *peace* is used as an adjective for a type of sacrifice (for example, "a peace offering") or as an expression of silence and contemplation (as in, "he held his peace"). In a few verses it is connected to other topics, which follow.

Joy

For ye shall go out with joy, and be led forth with peace: the mountains and the hills shall break forth before you into singing, and all the trees of the field shall clap their hands.

ISAIAH 55:12

Meekness

But the meek shall inherit the earth; and shall delight themselves in the abundance of peace.

PSALM 37:11

But thou, O man of God, flee these things; and follow after righteousness, godliness, faith, love, patience, meekness. Fight the good fight of faith, lay hold on eternal life, whereunto thou art also called, and hast professed a good profession before many witnesses.

1 TIMOTHY 6:11–12

Offerings

An altar of earth thou shalt make unto me, and shalt sacrifice thereon thy burnt offerings, and thy peace offerings, thy sheep, and thine oxen: in all places where I record my name I will come unto thee, and I will bless thee.

EXODUS 20:24

Prophecy

The prophet which prophesieth of peace, when the word of the prophet shall come to pass, then shall the prophet be known, that the LORD hath truly sent him.

JEREMIAH 28:9

And when he had opened the second seal, I heard the second beast say, Come and see. And there went out another horse that was red: and power was given to him that sat thereon to take peace from the earth, and that they should kill one another: and there was given unto him a great sword.

REVELATION 6:3–4

Righteousness

Mercy and truth are met together; righteousness and peace have kissed each other.

PSALM 85:10

And the work of righteousness shall be peace; and the effect of righteousness quietness and assurance forever.

ISAIAH 32:17

When a strong man armed keepeth his palace, his goods are in peace: But when a stronger than he shall come upon him, and overcome him, he taketh from him all his armour wherein he trusted, and divideth his spoils. He that is not with me is against me: and he that gathereth not with me scattereth.

LUKE 11:21–23

The Wicked

There is no peace, saith my God, to the wicked.

ISAIAH 57:21

Their feet run to evil, and they make haste to shed innocent blood: their thoughts are thoughts of iniquity; wasting and destruction are in their paths. The way of peace they know not; and there is no judgment in their goings: they have made them crooked paths: whosoever goeth therein shall not know peace.

ISAIAH 59:7–8

Wherefore I will bring the worst of the heathen, and they shall possess their houses: I will also make the pomp of the strong to cease; and their holy places shall be defiled. Destruction cometh; and they shall seek peace, and there shall be none.

EZEKIEL 7:24–25

Behold upon the mountains the feet of him that bringeth good tidings, that publisheth peace! O Judah, keep thy solemn feasts, perform thy vows: for the wicked shall no more pass through thee; he is utterly cut off.

NAHUM 1:15

As it is written, There is none righteous, no, not one: There is none that understandeth, there is none that seeketh after God. They are all gone out of the way, they are together become unprofitable; there is none that doeth good, no, not one. Their throat is an open sepulchre; with their tongues they have used deceit; the poison of asps is under their lips: Whose mouth is full of cursing and bitterness: Their feet are swift to shed blood: Destruction and misery are in their ways: And the way of peace have they not known: There is no fear of God before their eyes.

ROMANS 3:10–18

Wisdom

Happy is the man that findeth wisdom, and the man that getteth understanding. For the merchandise of it is better than the merchandise of silver, and the gain thereof than fine gold. She is more precious than rubies: and all the things thou canst desire are not to be compared unto her. Length of days is in her right hand; and in her left hand riches and honour. Her ways are ways of pleasantness, and all her paths are peace.

PROVERBS 3:13–17

Even a fool, when he holdeth his peace, is counted wise: and he that shutteth his lips is esteemed a man of understanding.

PROVERBS 17:28

But the wisdom that is from above is first pure, then peaceable, gentle, and easy to be intreated, full of mercy and good fruits, without partiality, and without hypocrisy.

JAMES 3:17

Praise thy Savior God that drew thee
To that cross, new life to give,
Held a blood sealed pardon to thee,
Bade thee look to Him and live.

Praise the grace whose threats alarmed thee,
Roused thee from thy fatal ease;
Praise the grace whose promise warmed thee,
Praise the grace that whispered peace.

FRANCIS SCOTT KEY

Peace
as a
Blessing

This concluding section is a collection of blessings that invoke the concept of peace. Considering the number of times this is seen through the pages of scripture, blessing another with the hope of peace is truly a godly endeavor.

Since the God of heaven has granted peace to the believer through the finished work of Jesus Christ, what greater service could the Christian provide than to grant peace in turn to a fellow believer or to an unbeliever in need of God's grace.

Perhaps you will consider adding this type of blessing as a gift to others as you walk with Jesus Christ.

To Abraham

And thou shalt go to thy fathers in peace; thou shalt be buried in a good old age.

GENESIS 15:15

To Jacob

And Jacob awaked out of his sleep, and he said, Surely the LORD is in this place; and I knew it not. And he was afraid, and said, How dreadful is this place! this is none other but the house of God, and this is the gate of heaven. And Jacob rose up early in the morning, and took the stone that he had put for his pillows, and set it up for a pillar, and poured oil upon the top of it. And he called the name of that place Bethel: but the name of that city was called Luz at the first. And Jacob vowed a vow, saying, If God will be with me, and will keep me in this way that I go, and will give me bread to eat, and raiment to put on, So that I come again to my father's house in peace; then shall the LORD be my God: And this stone, which I have set for a pillar, shall be God's house: and of all that thou shalt give me I will surely give the tenth unto thee.

GENESIS 28:16–22

To Pharaoh

And Joseph answered Pharaoh, saying, It is not in me: God shall give Pharaoh an answer of peace.

GENESIS 41:16

* * *

From Jethro to Moses

And Moses went and returned to Jethro his father in law, and said unto him, Let me go, I pray thee, and return unto my brethren which are in Egypt, and see whether they be yet alive. And Jethro said to Moses, Go in peace.

EXODUS 4:18

Aaron and his sons to the nation of Israel

Speak unto Aaron and unto his sons, saying, On this wise ye shall bless the children of Israel, saying unto them, The LORD bless thee, and keep thee: The LORD make his face shine upon thee, and be gracious unto thee: The LORD lift up his countenance upon thee, and give thee peace. And they shall put my name upon the children of Israel, and I will bless them.

NUMBERS 6:23–27

To Phinehas

Phinehas, the son of Eleazar, the son of Aaron the priest, hath turned my wrath away from the children of Israel, while he was zealous for my sake among them, that I consumed not the children of Israel in my jealousy. Wherefore say, Behold, I give unto him my covenant of peace: And he shall have it, and his seed after him, even the covenant of an everlasting priesthood; because he was zealous for his God, and made an atonement for the children of Israel.

NUMBERS 25:11–13

To Gideon

And when Gideon perceived that he was an angel of the LORD, Gideon said, Alas, O LORD God! for because I have seen an angel of the LORD face to face. And the LORD said unto him, Peace be unto thee; fear not: thou shalt not die. Then Gideon built an altar there unto the LORD, and called it Jehovah-shalom: unto this day it is yet in Ophrah of the Abiezrites.

JUDGES 6:22–24

A priest to the children of Dan

And the children of Dan sent of their family five men from their coasts, men of valour, from Zorah, and from Eshtaol, to spy out the land, and to search it; and they said unto them, Go, search the land: who when they came to mount Ephraim, to the house of Micah, they lodged there. When they were by the house of Micah, they knew the voice of the young man the Levite: and they turned in thither, and said unto him, Who brought thee hither? and what makest thou in this place? and what hast thou here? And he said unto them, Thus and thus dealeth Micah with me, and hath hired me, and I am his priest. And they said unto him, Ask counsel, we pray thee, of God, that we may know whether our way which we go shall be prosperous. And the priest said unto them, Go in peace: before the LORD is your way wherein ye go.

JUDGES 18:2–6

Hezekiah to Isaiah

Then said Hezekiah to Isaiah, Good is the word of the LORD which thou hast spoken. He said moreover, For there shall be peace and truth in my days.

ISAIAH 39:8

Isaiah to the righteous

The righteous perisheth, and no man layeth it to heart: and merciful men are taken away, none considering that the righteous is taken away from the evil to come. He shall enter into peace: they shall rest in their beds, each one walking in his uprightness.

ISAIAH 57:1–2

To Zedekiah

Yet hear the word of the LORD, O Zedekiah king of Judah; Thus saith the LORD of thee, Thou shalt not die by the sword: But thou shalt die in peace: and with the burnings of thy fathers, the former kings which were before thee, so shall they burn odours for thee; and they will lament thee, saying, Ah lord! for I have pronounced the word, saith the LORD.

JEREMIAH 34:4–5

King Nebuchadnezzar to all people

Nebuchadnezzar the king, unto all people, nations, and languages, that dwell in all the earth; Peace be multiplied unto you. I thought it good to shew the signs and wonders that the high God hath wrought toward me. How great are his signs! and how mighty are his wonders! His kingdom is an everlasting kingdom, and his dominion is from generation to generation.

DANIEL 4:1–3

King Darius to all people

Then king Darius wrote unto all people, nations, and languages, that dwell in all the earth; Peace be multiplied unto you.

DANIEL 6:25

A "man" to Daniel

Then there came again and touched me one like the appearance of a man, and he strengthened me, And said, O man greatly beloved, fear not: peace be unto thee, be strong, yea, be strong. And when he had spoken unto me, I was strengthened, and said, Let my lord speak; for thou hast strengthened me.

DANIEL 10:18–19

To the priests of Levi

And ye shall know that I have sent this commandment unto you, that my covenant might be with Levi, saith the LORD of hosts. My covenant was with him of life and peace; and I gave them to him for the fear wherewith he feared me, and was afraid before my name. The law of truth was in his mouth, and iniquity was not found in his lips: he walked with me in peace and equity, and did turn many away from iniquity.

MALACHI 2:5–6

Zacharias to his son, John

And thou, child, shalt be called the prophet of the Highest: for thou shalt go before the face of the Lord to prepare his ways; To give knowledge of salvation unto his people by the remission of their sins, Through the tender mercy of our God; whereby the dayspring from on high hath visited us, To give light to them that sit in darkness and in the shadow of death, to guide our feet into the way of peace.

LUKE 1:76–79

Jesus to the sea

And there arose a great storm of wind, and the waves beat into the ship, so that it was now full. And he was in the hinder part of the ship, asleep on a pillow: and they awake him, and say unto him, Master, carest thou not that we perish? And he arose, and rebuked the wind, and said unto the sea, Peace, be still. And the wind ceased, and there was a great calm. And he said unto them, Why are ye so fearful? how is it that ye have no faith? And they feared exceedingly, and said one to another, What manner of man is this, that even the wind and the sea obey him?

MARK 4:37–41

Jesus to a woman who had sinned

And he turned to the woman, and said unto Simon, Seest thou this woman? I entered into thine house, thou gavest me no water for my feet: but she hath washed my feet with tears, and wiped them with the hairs of her head. Thou gavest me no kiss: but this woman since the time I came in hath not ceased to kiss my feet. My head with oil thou didst not anoint: but this woman hath anointed my feet with ointment. Wherefore I say unto thee, Her sins, which are many, are forgiven; for she loved much: but to whom little is forgiven, the same loveth little. And he said unto her, Thy sins are forgiven. And they that sat at meat with him began to say within themselves, Who is this that forgiveth sins also? And he said to the woman, Thy faith hath saved thee; go in peace.

LUKE 7:44–50

Jesus to an ill woman who touched Him

And a woman having an issue of blood twelve years, which had spent all her living upon physicians, neither could be healed of any, Came behind him, and touched the border of his garment: and immediately her issue of blood stanched. And Jesus said, Who touched me? When all denied, Peter and they that were with him said, Master, the multitude throng thee and press thee, and sayest thou, Who touched me? And Jesus said, Somebody hath touched me: for I perceive that virtue is gone out of me. And when the woman saw that she was not hid, she came trembling, and falling down before him, she declared unto him before all the people for what cause she had touched him, and how she was healed immediately. And he said unto her, Daughter, be of good comfort: thy faith hath made thee whole; go in peace.

LUKE 8:43–48 (SEE ALSO MARK 5)

Jesus to His disciples, just prior to His arrest and death

Behold, the hour cometh, yea, is now come, that ye shall be scattered, every man to his own, and shall leave me alone: and yet I am not alone, because the Father is with me. These things I have spoken unto you, that in me ye might have peace. In the world ye shall have tribulation: but be of good cheer; I have overcome the world.

JOHN 16:32–33

Jesus to His disciples, after His resurrection

And as they thus spake, Jesus himself stood in the midst of them, and saith unto them, Peace be unto you. But they were terrified and affrighted, and supposed that they had seen a spirit. And he said unto them, Why are ye troubled? and why do thoughts arise in your hearts? Behold my hands and my feet, that it is I myself: handle me, and see; for a spirit hath not flesh and bones, as ye see me have. And when he had thus spoken, he shewed them his hands and his feet.

LUKE 24:36–40 (SEE ALSO JOHN 20)

Paul to the church in Rome

To all that be in Rome, beloved of God, called to be saints: Grace to you and peace from God our Father, and the Lord Jesus Christ.

ROMANS 1:7

Now the God of hope fill you with all joy and peace in believing, that ye may abound in hope, through the power of the Holy Ghost. Now the God of peace be with you all. Amen.

ROMANS 15:13, 33

Paul to the church in Corinth

Paul called to be an apostle of Jesus Christ through the will of God, and Sosthenes our brother, Unto the church of God which is at Corinth, to them that are sanctified in Christ Jesus, called to be saints, with all that in every place call upon the name of Jesus Christ our Lord, both their's and our's: Grace be unto you, and peace, from God our Father, and from the Lord Jesus Christ.

1 CORINTHIANS 1:1–3

Paul, an apostle of Jesus Christ by the will of God, and Timothy our brother, unto the church of God which is at Corinth, with all the saints which are in all Achaia: Grace be to you and peace from God our Father, and from the Lord Jesus Christ.

2 CORINTHIANS 1:1–2

Paul to the churches of Galatia

Paul, an apostle, (not of men, neither by man, but by Jesus Christ, and God the Father, who raised him from the dead;) And all the brethren which are with me, unto the churches of Galatia: Grace be to you and peace from God the Father, and from our Lord Jesus Christ, who gave himself for our sins, that he might deliver us from this present evil world, according to the will of God and our Father: To whom be glory for ever and ever. Amen.

GALATIANS 1:1–5

Paul to the church in Ephesus

Paul, an apostle of Jesus Christ by the will of God, to the saints which are at Ephesus, and to the faithful in Christ Jesus: Grace be to you, and peace, from God our Father, and from the Lord Jesus Christ.

EPHESIANS 1:1–2

Paul to the church in Philippi

Paul and Timotheus, the servants of Jesus Christ, to all the saints in Christ Jesus which are at Philippi, with the bishops and deacons: Grace be unto you, and peace, from God our Father, and from the Lord Jesus Christ. I thank my God upon every remembrance of you, Always in every prayer of mine for you all making request with joy, For your fellowship in the gospel from the first day until now; Being confident of this very thing, that he which hath begun a good work in you will perform it until the day of Jesus Christ:

PHILIPPIANS 1:1–6

Paul to the church in Colosse

Paul, an apostle of Jesus Christ by the will of God, and Timotheus our brother, To the saints and faithful brethren in Christ which are at Colosse: Grace be unto you, and peace, from God our Father and the Lord Jesus Christ. We give thanks to God and the Father of our Lord Jesus Christ, praying always for you.

COLOSSIANS 1:1–3

Paul to the church at Thessalonica

Paul, and Silvanus, and Timotheus, unto the church of the Thessalonians which is in God the Father and in the Lord Jesus Christ: Grace be unto you, and peace, from God our Father, and the Lord Jesus Christ. We give thanks to God always for you all, making mention of you in our prayers; Remembering without ceasing your work of faith, and labour of love, and patience of hope in our Lord Jesus Christ, in the sight of God and our Father; knowing, brethren beloved, your election of God.

1 Thessalonians 1:1–3

(see also 2 Thessalonians 1)

Paul to Timothy

Paul, an apostle of Jesus Christ by the commandment of God our Saviour, and Lord Jesus Christ, which is our hope; Unto Timothy, my own son in the faith: Grace, mercy, and peace, from God our Father and Jesus Christ our Lord.

1 TIMOTHY 1:1–2
(SEE ALSO 2 TIMOTHY 1, TITUS 1:4,
AND PHILEMON 3)

Peter to the scattered church

Peter, an apostle of Jesus Christ, to the strangers scattered throughout Pontus, Galatia, Cappadocia, Asia, and Bithynia, Elect according to the foreknowledge of God the Father, through sanctification of the Spirit, unto obedience and sprinkling of the blood of Jesus Christ: Grace unto you, and peace, be multiplied. Blessed be the God and Father of our Lord Jesus Christ, which according to his abundant mercy hath begotten us again unto a lively hope by the resurrection of Jesus Christ from the dead, to an inheritance incorruptible, and undefiled, and that fadeth not away, reserved in heaven for you, Who are kept by the power of God through faith unto salvation ready to be revealed in the last time.

1 PETER 1:1–5 (SEE ALSO 2 PETER 1)

The elder (John) to the elect lady and her children

Grace be with you, mercy, and peace, from God the Father, and from the Lord Jesus Christ, the Son of the Father, in truth and love.

2 JOHN 3

❦

The elder (John) to Gaius

But I trust I shall shortly see thee, and we shall speak face to face. Peace be to thee. Our friends salute thee. Greet the friends by name.

3 JOHN 14

Jude to the "sanctified" and "preserved"

Jude, the servant of Jesus Christ, and brother of James, to them that are sanctified by God the Father, and preserved in Jesus Christ, and called: Mercy unto you, and peace, and love, be multiplied.

JUDE 1–2

John to the seven churches in Asia

John to the seven churches which are in Asia: Grace be unto you, and peace, from him which is, and which was, and which is to come; and from the seven Spirits which are before his throne; And from Jesus Christ, who is the faithful witness, and the first begotten of the dead, and the prince of the kings of the earth. Unto him that loved us, and washed us from our sins in his own blood, And hath made us kings and priests unto God and his Father; to him be glory and dominion for ever and ever. Amen.

REVELATION 1:4–6

Night's shadows falling men
    to rest are calling;
Rest we, possessing heav'nly
    peace and blessing:
This we implore Thee,
    falling down before Thee,
Great King of Glory!

O Lord of Glory, praise we
    and adore Thee—
Thee for us given, our true
    Rest from Heaven!
Rest, peace, and blessing,
    we are now possessing,
Thy Name confessing.

ARTHUR T. RUSSELL

Final Thoughts

*For I know the thoughts
that I think toward you, saith the LORD,
thoughts of peace, and not of evil,
to give you an expected end.*
JEREMIAH 29:11

We hear much of "peace" at Christmastime—though around the globe soldiers are fighting, civic leaders are arguing, and our fellow citizens are contending for parking spaces and popular products at the mall. Is peace really possible in this world?

Yes—but only on God's terms. Though He offers peace to all, not everyone accepts the gift. True peace is reserved for followers of Jesus—an inner peace in a world of turmoil, and an eternity of peace in God's world to come.

Jesus' promises to His own

Peace I leave with you, my peace I give unto you: not as the world giveth, give I unto you. Let not your heart be troubled, neither let it be afraid.

JOHN 14:27

These things I have spoken unto you, that in me ye might have peace. In the world ye shall have tribulation: but be of good cheer; I have overcome the world.

JOHN 16:33

Christmas Stories
for Bedtime

For spiritual "quality time" with your five- to eight-year-old kids this holiday season, check out *Christmas Stories for Bedtime*—going a step beyond the traditional storybook! Thirty readings are included, in fun, easy-to-understand stories that your kids will love. From Old Testament prophecies of the Messiah, to the actual Nativity and all the details that surrounded it, *Christmas Stories for Bedtime* explains the first Christmas in ways that young hearts can grasp. Each chapter is accompanied by full-color illustration and design, making *Christmas Stories for Bedtime* an ideal book for learning and fun.

ISBN 978-1-60260-652-4